ACKNOWLEDGMENTS

This book was
built with guidance
from Peter Ernerk,
Nunavut's Deputy
Minister of
Culture, Language, Elders and Youth;
and Norman Hallendy, fellow of the Nunavut Research Institute,
the Canadian Museum of Civilization and the Smithsonian Institution, research associate of
the Arctic Institute of North America and director of the Tukilik Foundation.
Photographs were contributed by Nunavut Tourism,
the National Archives, Peter Ernerk and
John MacDonald (Nunavut Research Institute).
Thanks to Rosemarie Kuptana (Inuit path to self-determination),
Lyndsay Green (Inukshuk Project), Barb Bolin
(Haliburton School of Fine Arts), Doug Stenton
(Inuit Heritage Trust), Marion Soublière (Nunavut
Handbook) and Tamilik's Inuktitut Services.
Information about inuksuit was derived from a number of sources.
These include: Allan Angmarlik's (Inuit Heritage Trust) interviews

with Inuit elders Adamie Nukiguak,
Ulaayuruluk and Simo Alookie;
with Rosie Iqallijuq (shaman
of Igloolik; Francois Quassa's
Louis Tapardjuk (Igloolik
Nunavut Research Institute);
letters and stories
him by his parents);
account of women
Norman Hallendy's
years with Inuit elders

George Kappianaq, Abraham
John MacDonald's interview
story), the eldest resident
interview, translated by
Inullariit Elders Society and
Peter Ernerk's articles,
(Aningaat story as told to
Rasmussen's 1930
lost at sea; and
work over many
throughout the Arctic.

THE Inuksuk BOOK

ᐃᓄᒃᓱᐊᓄᑦ

Mary Wallace

MAPLE
TREE
PRESS

Maple Tree Press Inc.
51 Front Street East, Suite 200, Toronto, Ontario M5E 1B3
www.mapletreepress.com

Text and Illustrations © 1999 Mary Wallace
Introduction © 1999 Norman Hallendy

Distributed in Canada by Raincoast Books
9050 Shaughnessy Street, Vancouver, British Columbia
V6P 6E5

Distributed in the United States by Publishers Group West
1700 Fourth Street, Berkeley, California 94710

We acknowledge the generous support of the Canada Council for the Arts and the Ontario Arts Council for our publishing program.

Dedication
To all our children

Cataloguing in Publication Data
Wallace, Mary, 1950-
        The Inuksuk book

Includes index.
ISBN 1-897066-13-9

1. Inuit—Canada—Material culture—Juvenile literature.
2. Inuit—Canada—Social life and customs—Juvenile literature.
I. Title.

E99.E7W345 2004   j305'.897'12071   C2004-901567-2

Design & art direction: Word & Image Design Studio

Printed in China

H   I   J   K

Photo Credits
Front cover photograph: Heringa, Dan/NT*; 3: Moodie, J.D./NAC*, C-1827; 4–5: Ernerk, Peter; 6 (inset): NAC, C-37124; 6–7: Bell, R./NAC, C-86363; 8–9: MacDonald, John; 10–11 (background): NT/H2414; 11 (inset): Beedel, Mike/NT; 12–13: Harrington, Richard/NAC, PA-114652; 12 (inset): NT/A2058; 14–15 (background): Ernerk, P.; 16: Weber, Wolfgang/NT; 17: Ernerk, P.; 18–19 (background): Ernerk, P.; 20–21: NAC, C-35377; 21 (inset): Anderson, Rudolph M./NAC, PA-127411; 22–23 (background): Ernerk, P.; 23 (inset): MacDonald, J.; 24–25: McKeand, D.L./NAC, PA-102197; 24 (inset): Macintosh, T./NT; 26–27 (background): NAC, PA-66622; 27 (inset): MacDonald, J.; 28: Harrington, R./NAC, PA-166830; 29: Harrington, R./NAC, PA-114727; 30–31 (background): Finnie, R.S./NAC, PA-101171; 31 (inset): Harrington, R./NAC, PA-138024; 32–33: Harrington, R./NAC, PA-129873; 32 (inset): Macintosh, T./NT; 34–35 (background): Ernerk, P.; 35 (inset): Ernerk, P.; 36–37: Harringon, R./NAC, PA-114685; 37 (inset): Douglas, George Mellis/NAC, PA 145220; 38–39 (background): Harrington, R./NAC, PA-129589; 40–41: Burwash, L.T./NAC, PA-99306; 41 (inset): NAC, PA-47999; 42–43 (background): Gilliat, Rosemary/NAC, PA-145050; 44: Robinson, J.L./NAC, PA-102212; 45: NAC, C-30174; 46–47 (background): Harrington, R./NAC, PA-114682; 47 (inset): Ernerk, P.; 48–49: Finnie, R.S./NAC, PA-101233; 49 (inset): Ernerk, P.; 50–51 (background): MacDonald, J.; 51 (inset): NAC, PA-13011; 52–53: Harrington, R./NAC, PA-129935; 52 (inset): Harrington, R./NAC, PA-147271; 54–55 (background): MacDonald, J.; 55 (inset): NT/H106; 56–57: MacDonald, J.; 56 (inset): Burwash, L.T./NAC, PA-99068; all photos on pages 58–61: Wallace, Mary, except 59 (inset), MacDonald, J.; 62–63: Tyrell, Joseph B./NAC, C-30219.

*NT = Nunavut Tourism; NAC = the National Archives of Canada

·CONTENTS

Left: Inuit women stand against the arctic landscape, well protected in waterproof parkas. *Below:* An inuksuk that shows where meat is stored.

INTRODUCTION
BY NORMAN HALLENDY

I have two names. The name my mother and father gave me is Norman and the name the people in Cape Dorset gave me is Apirsuqti (pronounced a-peer-sook-ti), which means "the inquisitive one." They gave me that name because I was always asking questions so that I could learn things from them about nature, animals and people, and how they lived in the Arctic.

The ancestors of my northern friends have lived in the Arctic for over 4,000 years. Their descendants today call themselves Inuit, which means "human beings." In the past, they lived completely with nature. Everything they had came from the sea or the land. They made all they needed to stay alive from stone, and the bone, skin and ivory they got from the animals they hunted. Nothing was wasted; everything was valuable in some way.

To survive, the Inuit had to hunt all the time: in summer and in winter, in good and bad weather. They had to hunt in many places at different times of the year because the animals they needed arrived there at various times. It was necessary to travel long distances in order to get enough food, especially in early times before the Inuit had rifles.

One of the most important things the Inuit made were called *inuksuit*. The singular is *inuksuk*. This word means "thing that can act in the place of a human being." We are familiar with things that work in similar ways. For example, a scarecrow acts like a human being when it frightens away birds. A traffic light tells you when to stop or go in place of a police officer. A statue tells you that a person is being remembered. An arrow nailed to a tree tells you which direction to go. Inuksuit are like these, but far more important, because they have helped save lives in the harsh arctic environment. They could be used to help in many different ways, but the five most important were: to show the way when travellers were a long way from home; to warn of very dangerous places; to show where food was stored (especially when covered with snow); to show where a significant thing happened and therefore where people should act respectful; and, most important, to act as helpers for hunting caribou.

The caribou was the most important land animal for the Inuit. In the old days when Inuit hunted with only bow and arrows, they built inuksuit of stones and placed them upon the land in such a way as to frighten the caribou and guide them straight toward the waiting hunters. In this way, the inuksuit became part of the hunting party. They did the work of humans even though they were made of stone.

Stones come in many different shapes. Inuksuit use three basic shapes. There are round stones called boulders. About all you can do with these is pile them up. There are thin, flat stones, which you can stack like books into a few different shapes. And then there are chunks of broken rock. You can stack the broken rock or balance other pieces on top. You can make them into many more shapes than you can with boulders or flat rocks. Most of the inuksuit in the Arctic are made from broken rock because there is something special about using it—it is the easiest to balance.

The stones to make an inuksuk were carefully chosen so that they could stand or lie upon one another without falling, no matter how fierce a storm. There are inuksuit that have been standing in the Arctic for hundreds of years, probably even longer. You can tell if an inuksuk is very old if you see it covered in lichens. Lichens grow in most places in the world, and in most places in the Arctic. Because they take such a long time to grow, it means that the thing they are growing upon is also very old. I have seen many inuksuit so covered in lichens that they look as if they are wearing coats.

These ancient inuksuit tell us that the Inuit were in Arctic North America long before the arrival of people from other lands, except the native peoples who lived much farther to the south. Such old inuksuit are treated with great respect because they remind the Inuit of their ancestors. Even now, they can show the way to good hunting places, they can guide you when you are in a strange place, they can warn you of danger just ahead and they can fill your heart with joy when you stand beside them at a very beautiful place. In this way, an inuksuk is a gift from the past that keeps giving to anyone who comes its way.

When you look at an old inuksuk you are seeing more than just a stack of stones. You are seeing the thoughts of another person left upon the land, as you see the thoughts of another person in the words you read in a book. Because the Inuit had no written language until quite recently, storytelling and such things as inuksuit were the ways that information was passed on from one generation to another.

One of my Inuit teachers explained why it was so important to remember the shape of every inuksuk and the look of the land I saw whenever I was travelling. By doing this I could make a map in my head of my journey. It was possible for one person to tell another person how to get from one distant place to another by describing not only the landscape but the shapes of the inuksuit along the way.

Like humans, inuksuit have different names. Their special names reflect their distinct purposes, which is how people can know what the inuksuk is telling them. For example, one of the most important of all the inuksuit is called *nangiarautimik qaujimalitaq*, which is an inuksuk that warns you of great danger. So if I carefully described an inuksuk you would meet on your travels as a *nangiarautimik qaujimalitaq*, you would know you were entering a very dangerous place. In the south we have many signs without words. They act in the same way, by telling us certain things, such as: "Do not enter here;" "This is the way to go;" "Be careful," and so on.

There are stone figures made by the Inuit that look like a person. Sometimes they look so real you think they are people off in the distance. The name of this kind of stone figure is an *inunnguaq*. Its name means "that which looks like a person." An inuksuk can have all kinds of different shapes, but an *inunnguaq* always looks like a human being. Some are very old and were built to show someone's thanks for living in such a beautiful place. Others were built to tell strangers that people were living in the area. Some were built to show respect for a person who had died and was much loved.

Things that we might call inuksuit were built all over the world in ancient times. They just had different names because they were built by people who spoke other languages. These stone figures, like the ones built by the Inuit, were helpers to the early hunters and travellers. Except for a very few places in the world, these ancient helpers are gone and now forgotten. But in the Arctic, they still stand and remind us of the first people who made the Arctic their home. If inuksuit could speak, they would tell us stories of the time when humans were a part of nature and not yet so separated from it as we have come to be. Today, inuksuit are still being built in the North. In this book you will discover more about these special and very beautiful structures.

Norman Hallendy has travelled throughout the Arctic for over thirty years. He has studied inuksuit and written about the many things he's learned from Inuit elders, which has earned him an international reputation as an expert on the subject. He is a research fellow of the Arctic Institute of North America, the Canadian Museum of Civilization, the Nunavut Research Institute and the Smithsonian Institution, as well as the director of the Tukilik Foundation, which is dedicated to deepening our understanding of the Canadian Arctic. Norman Hallendy is the author and photographer of a book on inuksuit called *The Silent Messengers*.

ᐅᖃᖅ

NUNAVUT
OUR LAND

The land of the North: barren but beautiful, peaceful yet powerful. Endless horizons stretch out across the treeless tundra. There are no cities, no crowds, no polluting noises. The circle of seasons changes the long darkness of the arctic winter into the all-day-and-night shimmering brightness of the summer sun. The mystery and richness of life here are secrets closely linked to the land, secrets that can be only slowly and carefully discovered.

Arctic Canada consists of about one-third of the geographic land space of the nation. In 1999, a large Inuit land-claim settlement created a new territory within Arctic Canada, called Nunavut. Nunavut means "our land" in Inuktitut, the language of the Inuit. This new territory, in which the North Magnetic Pole is located, is notorious for having the coldest weather in Canada. Nunavut sits on the ancient rocks of the Canadian Shield and has many islands, bays and channels. It is a place where the mountains, ice and snow blend into the sea and sky.

Above: Flowers bloom across the treeless tundra, signalling that spring has come to the Arctic.

For thousands of years, Arctic North America has been the home of the Inuit. Plural for Inuk, Inuit is the Inuktitut word for "human beings." Today, Inuit make up most of the population of Nunavut, spanning at least three generations.

The elders are the older Inuit, who speak mainly Inuktitut. They were born on the land and have lived on the land for most of their lives. They are respected for their wisdom and their knowledge of the traditional Inuit way of life.

Most middle-aged Inuit are bilingual, able to speak English and Inuktitut. They are familiar with both the Inuit and non-Inuit world. They may have lived on the land, but are also familiar with life in a settlement. This generation is the link between the old and the new.

Many of the younger Inuit were born and raised within the boundaries of their community and have gone to school for most of their lives. They speak mainly English, but are taught Inuktitut in school and at home. Young Inuit strive to find the balance between the contemporary world and traditional Inuit values, such as respect for the land, the sea and the animals.

Above: Glorious summertime in the Arctic. *Right:* Inuit hunters look out across the frozen tundra in the mid-1900s.

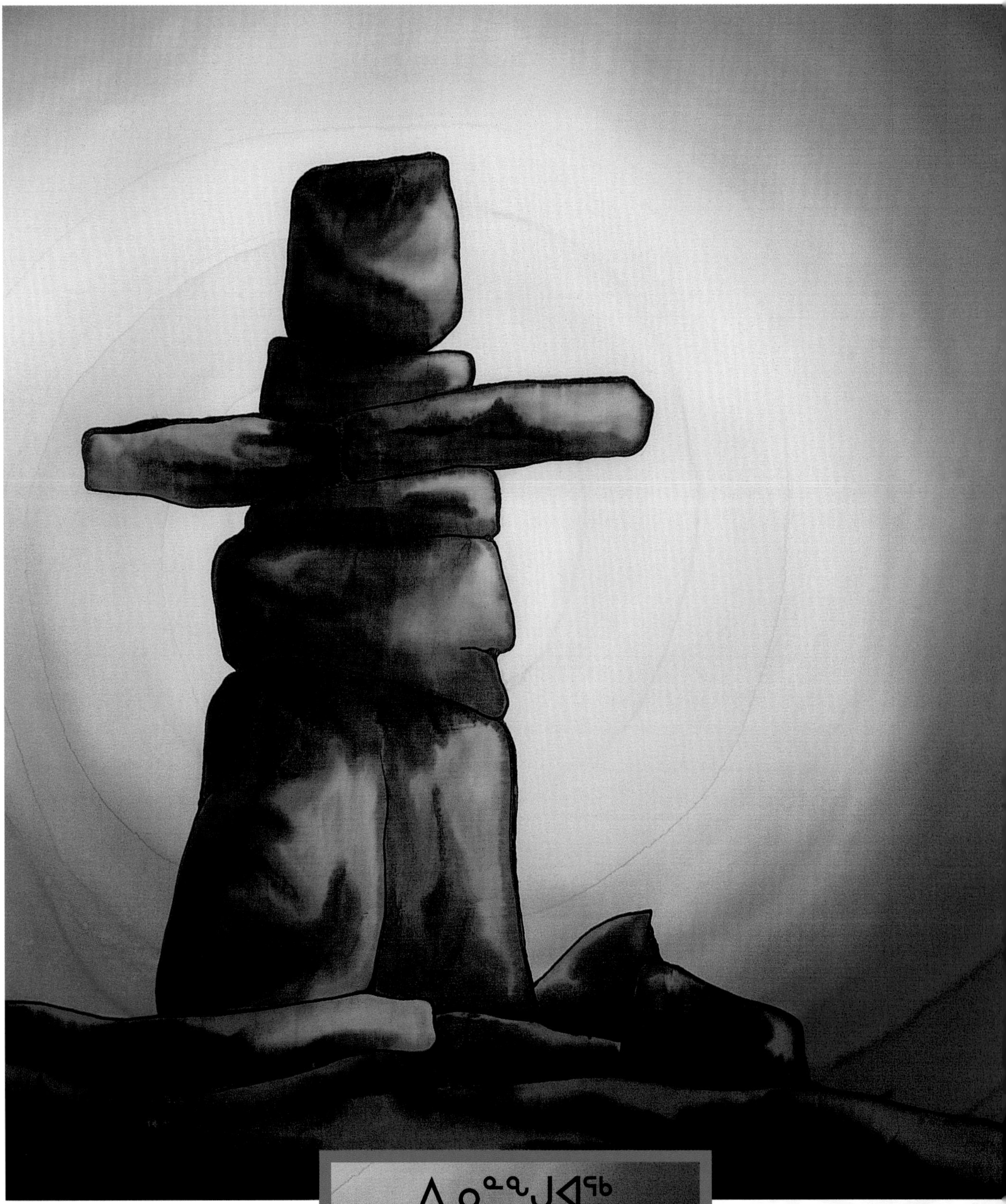

ᐃᓄᖕᖑᐊᖅ

INUNNGUAQ
LIKE A PERSON

An inuksuk is a stone structure that can communicate knowledge essential for survival to an Arctic traveller. Inuksuit (plural) are found throughout the Arctic areas of Alaska, Arctic Canada and Greenland. Inuksuit have been used by the Inuit to act in place of human messengers. For those who understand their forms, inuksuit in the Arctic are very important helpers: they can show direction, tell about a good hunting or fishing area, show where food is stored, indicate a good resting place or act as a message centre.

Every inuksuk is unique because it is built from the stones at hand. Inuksuit can be small or large; a single rock put in place; several rocks balanced on top of each other; boulders placed in a pile; or flat stones stacked. One of these stone structures is known as an inuksuk, two are called inuksuuk and three or more are referred to as inuksuit.

An inuksuk is a strong connection to the land: it is built on the land, it is made of the land and it tells about the land. Inuit are taught to be respectful of inuksuit. There is a traditional law, which persists today, that forbids damaging or destroying inuksuit in any way. New inuksuit can be built to mark the presence of modern-day Inuit, but the old ones should never be touched. Traditionally, it is said that if one destroys an inuksuk, his or her life will be cut shorter.

Left: An *inunnguaq* that has been built in more recent times. *Above:* These inuksuit tell where Inuit have travelled.

Over time, the style of building inuksuit has changed. In the past, most inuksuit were built by stacking rock in a particular way, but usually not in the shape of a human. However, many modern inuksuit are built to look like human figures made of stone (with a head, body, arms and legs). In Inuktitut, these are called *inunnguaq*. Some Inuit believe that this type of stone figure was first built about one hundred years ago, after the arrival of the *qallunaat* (non-Inuit) whalers. Others say that this human look-alike originated long before this century.

All things change with time; Inuit ways are not exempt. Today, as traditional ways are changing into contemporary ways Inuit, and even non-Inuit, sometimes build inuksuit simply to mark their presence—both in the Arctic and in their travels outside of their homeland.

ᓂᐅᕝᐹᖅᑕᕐᔪᐊᑦ

Niugvaliruluit
That has legs

The cold climate and rugged terrain make the Arctic a challenging place to travel in. Those who do are guided on their journey by inuksuit that stand along the way. These landmarks can show the way forward, as well as the safest and best routes home.

Years ago, knowledge of these routes was passed on orally. An Inuk could tell another how to travel across vast distances by describing the landscape and the various shapes of the inuksuit along the way. One man told of travelling almost 2,000 km (over 1,200 miles) guided by a song his father taught him describing the inuksuit he should look out for that would mark his way.

Inuksuit built with sighting holes in their middle are used for navigation. Each one points to one farther along the way. By looking through the window toward the next inuksuk, a traveller is guided along a travel route. These large inuksuit can be seen from far-off distances. Smaller ones are spaced so that one is visible from the last.

Along the journey, different inuksuit tell the traveller valuable information about the route: the depth of snow, where there is a safe crossing place or deep spots in a river, where there are good hunting areas and where to find landing sites for a kayak (*qajaq*). Two different-sized stones placed a small distance apart can act as an arrow indicating which direction should be taken. Inuksuit with two small arms can point to ideal routes, usually through low-lying valleys, which are the best way to travel to distant places. An inuksuk with its sighting hole at the bottom also indicates a safe passage to follow through a valley, helping the traveller avoid steep hills and impassable routes.

One Inuit legend tells about a blind boy named Aningaat. In the story, he asks his younger sister to bring him to a nearby pond where two loon spirits are swimming. At the pond, Aningaat tells his sister to go back to their tent, but to build *inuksukkat* (smaller inuksuit) on the way so that when he is able to see, he can find his way home. After his sister leaves, the loon spirits lick his eyes three times. After each lick, they ask him whether or not he can see. After the first two licks, his eyes are still foggy. But after the third lick, Aningaat can see so well that he can see even the smallest holes in the mountains across the pond. And so, with clear and happy sight, Aningaat can return home by following the *inuksukkat* that his little sister has built.

Above: A caribou-skin tent offers protection for two Copper Inuit families in the early 1900s. *Below:* The inuksuk in the centre guides these travellers to their summer camp in 1915.

ᓇᖅᑳᑕᐃᑦ

NAKKATAIT

THINGS THAT FELL INTO THE WATER

Hunting and fishing is an age-old way of life that endures among the Inuit. By tradition, Inuit live in harmony with nature. What's on the land and in the sea is there for them to take only as they need. Animals are never abused, and are treated with great respect. They are hunted only to provide the necessities of life: tools, food, clothing and shelter. What the Inuit have, they share with their fellow Inuit. It is this food-sharing system that has enabled them to survive many harsh winters.

In the seasonal cycle of traditional Inuit life, hunting, fishing and gathering meant travelling great distances across the land and sea to harvest enough game to survive. During the winter, Inuit crossed ice and snow to areas where there were caribou and seal. In the spring, they moved toward rivers to fish. By summer, much of the ice would have melted and hunting and fishing could be done by kayak. When fall came, Inuit would return to the coast to do more hunting and fishing. Even after the ice formed on the lakes, Inuit continued to fish by drilling holes in the ice. Whatever the season, inuksuit led the way to the best places to find meat and fish to eat.

Right: A hunter waits to harpoon a seal—an essential source of food and fuel during the long winter months—through a hole in the ice.

Foods traditionally eaten by Inuit are called *niqiit*, which means "meats." They include seal, walrus, whale (the skin is a delicacy called *maktaaq*) and caribou. Some of the seasonal foods were clams, partridge, berries, arctic char, lake trout, turbot, arctic hare and whale blubber. Most foods were eaten raw, frozen, dried, boiled or aged. Meat that is eaten raw is more nutritious and gives more energy than cooked meat.

Around lakes where Inuit fish, there are often two or three small inuksuit indicating the good fishing spots. Some of these inuksuit are constructed using two stones. The smaller stone is placed closer to the shore and points to where a fishing hole should be made on the frozen lake. The distance between the stones corresponds to the distance between the shoreline and where the fishing hole should be.

When a hunter kills a seal, it sinks to the bottom and two stones are used to indicate the location where the seal went down. This way a hunter will know exactly where to retrieve the sunken seal. In traditional times, winter subsistence depended on the seal because many other animals were hibernating or had migrated. A seal's meat and blubber were necessary for winter food and fuel for light and heat.

Above: Modern Inuit fishermen show their catch. *Full page:* These fishermen in the 1930s spear arctic char they have diverted into a trap built of stones.

ᑐᐸᖅᑲᒐᓗᐃᑦ

TUPJAKANGAUT
FOOTPRINTS OF GAME

Tupjakangaut is an important inuksuk because it steers hunters toward a good place to hunt caribou. These inuksuit usually stand amidst a perpetual layer of lichens and mosses. Caribou are attracted to these areas because mosses and lichens are a major source of food for grazing. Caribou live in small herds, with cows, calves and a few bulls, grazing on the tundra from spring to late summer. As winter approaches, they gather in large herds and migrate south to warmer climates.

In Inuktitut, caribou are known as *tuktut*. For a very long time, the lives of the Arctic people were intimately linked to these precious animals. In years when there were few caribou to hunt, Inuit faced cold, hungry and frightening winters. However, when caribou were plentiful, Inuit were warm, well fed and content.

Right: Caribou skin, both warm and light, was considered ideal for winter clothing.

Left: An Inuit girl in 1950 prepares a hide to make clothing by cleaning the underside with an ulu (a crescent-shaped knife). *Right:* An Inuit baby stays cozy inside her mother's parka in the mid-1900s.

When hunted, no part of the caribou was wasted. The meat was used for food, fat for candles, bone for tools, sinew for sewing and hides for trousers, coats, footwear, mittens, diapers, bedding and summer tents. The unique structure of the caribou's hollow hair makes its fur extremely warm, supple and light, as well as comfortable to wear. Babies wore only diapers made from caribou skin. To stay snug and safe, they were kept next to their mother's skin under several layers of caribou-hide clothing. The outer layer, called a parka, had a hood that was big enough for the baby's face to peek out beside its mother's.

Caribou hide was prepared by scraping off any fat and extra membranes using an ulu, then dried in the sun. Clothing patterns were cut from the hide with the ulu, and sewn together with thread made by twisting together thin strips of caribou sinew. A young child's outfit was often constructed from a single caribou hide. The back of the jacket matched the back line of the caribou, the hood was shaped from the head of the caribou and the child's sleeves and pant legs from the legs of the hide. For the Inuit, the soft and warm protective hide of the caribou covering the child represented a magical connection between the two.

ᐊᐅᑕᓐ ᖅᑯᑦ

Aulaqut
Makes things run away

Early fall is the best time to hunt caribou, when the caribou are fat and their hides are the right thickness for clothing. When the caribou appeared, Inuit traditionally believed that the animals had come to offer themselves to the waiting hunters. Inuit hunters were grateful to the caribou, and felt fortunate when they were able to hunt a large herd. They pursued, caught and killed the caribou as swiftly and painlessly as possible. Successful hunters did not brag; they were simply thankful.

One of the most important types of inuksuit are those that helped in the caribou hunt. These inuksuit were usually built with two or three rocks piled up. Converging lines of evenly spaced inuksuit were laid out along the migration route of a caribou herd. Arctic heather was inserted in between the rocks so that the long, wavy tendrils blew in the wind like human hair, making the inuksuit seem alive. When they saw them, the caribou would be spooked by these "scarecrows" and begin to stampede. The way the rocks had

Above: An Inuit hunter with a bow in the Coppermine District, Northwest Territories, in the mid-1900s.

Above: Dance of the Nattilik Inuit. *Right:* Inuksuit stand ready to channel caribou toward waiting hunters.

been set up led the running caribou toward a place where hunters waited behind boulders with bows and arrows. By tradition, when a group of caribou passed, a hunter was to shoot only the last animal, so that other waiting hunters would have a chance to shoot the remaining caribou.

Inuksuit built beside a lake prevented herds of migrating caribou from swimming into the lake, where they would spread out and be more difficult to hunt. An inuksuk row could also lead the caribou to a place more accessible to the hunters. When caribou were herded into water, they were hunted with kayaks and lances.

A successful hunt meant that there would be enough meat to enjoy at celebrations. Each celebration includes a huge feast. Inuit believe that all food tastes better when it is shared with family and friends. At a feast, stories and songs are exchanged, games are played, strangers become friends and there is much laughter.

ᖃᔭᖅᑯᓯᑦ

Qajakkuviit
Kayak rests

Inuit were dependent on the animals they hunted for their survival, which meant they always had to be where arctic game was close. When the game moved, the Inuit moved. Always travelling, Inuit often lived in temporary hunting camps. There they would build inuksuit by stacking rocks from around their camp into tall towers. Meat, dog harnesses and caribou skins were placed on top of these towers to be kept out of reach of hungry animals, such as wolves, polar bears and sled dogs. Larger dog sleds and kayaks were also placed upon rock towers. They would be laid upside down across two tall inuksuuk built side by side.

During the summer, there was more to hunt, so meat was generally more plentiful. That meant that very little food was carried from one camp to another. Instead, any extra meat was dried and stored. Similar, but smaller, stone inuksuit were used for drying fish and other meats. A line would be strung between two rock pillars, and thin strips cut from the meat were hung along this line to dry in the arctic sun. The dried meat would then be ready to store for a time when it was needed.

A well-balanced tower of skilfully chosen stones can stand up to the forces of wind and snow, sometimes for hundreds of years.

Full page: This woman, photo-graphed in the 1950s, is drying fish to feed her family during the long winter months. *Far right:* A kayak supported by inuksuuk on the shore of a lake.

Temporary camps were moved frequently, depending on the luck of the hunt. While the men spent most of their time hunting and fishing, the women looked after the very small children and cleaned and preserved the meat and fish. Older children were free to explore and play.

ᐱᒪᖅᑲᖅᓯᐱᑦ

PIRUJAQARVIK
WHERE THE MEAT CACHE IS

The Arctic environment can be cruel, especially during the dark winter months. Over the centuries, Inuit developed many ingenious ways to survive.

In traditional times, Inuit saved as much food as possible since meat was often scarce during the winter, when most of the animals the Inuit hunted either hibernated or migrated south. After a successful hunt, extra meat was cleaned, dried or left to ripen and placed in a low spot to store for retrieval at a later date. Lots of stones were piled on top of this meat cache to preserve it and hide it from hungry predators, such as foxes, wolves and polar bears. Then an inuksuk was built on a nearby high spot to act as a marker pointing toward the stored food.

In the winter, Inuit could retrieve this meat when they needed it. Even after a layer of snow had covered the food cache and dramatically changed the appearance of the landscape, the Inuit would be able to find the stash. The nearby inuksuk would be tall enough to rise above the snow and still be visible from a great distance.

The arctic landscape is covered by snow and ice for more than half the year. The snow is firm and dense, making it ideal for travelling by dog sled. This type of sled can travel fast, as well as haul heavy loads across wind-packed snow.

It can be difficult to find wood in the Far North, above the timberline. If there was no wood available to make sled runners, Inuit would improvise with a block of ice. Sometimes, they might even make runners by laying fish end to end and rolling them up in a wet caribou hide. After being tightly lashed together, the runners would be frozen into position and coated with a layer of ice to give them a smooth sliding surface. These sled runners were doubly useful because, if need be, they could even be eaten.

Right: Inuit women tying up blubber to be stored for the summer. *Full page:* A heavily laden sled makes its way through ice and snow in 1926.

ᐃᓄᒃᓱᒃ ᖃᐅᔨᐊᕈᑕᐅᖅ

INUKSUK QUVIASUKTUQ
INUKSUK EXPRESSING JOY

Sometimes an inuksuk is built simply as an expression of joy. An Inuk might show gratitude to the land by building an *inunnguaq*. Standing amidst a field of spring flowers, this happy *inunnguaq* might mark an excellent camping site.

Summer camps are usually built on high ground. From here, the view is excellent, and arctic breezes help keep away the swarms of spring and summer insects. At this time of year, the tundra is a vast and radiantly colored flower garden. The brilliant blooms of the purple saxifrage flower begin to appear. The gentle fragrance of the Lapland rose bay mingles with that of arctic heather. Tiny yellow mountain aven flower heads follow the sun as it crosses along the northern sky. Roots of arctic poppies, lupines, dandelions, daisies and harebells drink the melted ice water as it seeps through a thin layer of thawed soil. Bear berries, crowberries, blueberries and cranberries stand ready to be harvested. This luxuriant growth of plants provides food for the insects, birds and other plant-eating animals of the Arctic. Certain plants also are used by the Inuit for food, fuel and medicine.

Left: Inuit girls brew a pot of tea, mid-1900s. *Above:* Picking berries on the tundra in the early 1900s.

When the summer sun warms the land, melt water collects in clear pools that lie just above the permafrost, a layer of earth that never thaws in these far northern regions. This clean water can be enjoyed for drinking, as well as for swimming.

A delicious warm pot of tea is often made at a summer camp. After collecting a pile of branches from an arctic heather shrub, an Inuk lights a fire, adds a few rocks to hold extra heat and quickly brings a cooking pot of melted ice water to a boil. Labrador tea, a plant that is collected from the tundra, is added to the pot. Soon this refreshing and soothing drink is ready to be shared among fellow campers.

ᐃᑯᒃᓯᒃ ᐊᓂᖅᓂᑕᒃ

Inuksuk Anirnilik
Inuksuk with a spirit

S ometimes inuksuit are built out of respect for a much-loved person, serving as a memorial to that person's spirit. One Inuit story tells of inuksuit that were built along the shore of a bay as memorials to women who drowned near there. It is told that many years ago, the men of an Inuit community went away hunting. While they were gone, the women went out onto the sea ice to fish for salmon. But spring was coming, and the winter ice was beginning to melt. Suddenly, the ice that the women were on broke from the shore and began to drift away. Only one woman dared to jump ashore. The rest were carried out to sea and drowned. When the men returned, their grief was great. They built an inuksuk for each drowned woman because they wanted the women's souls to be on dry land, and not out in the wet sea.

In traditional Inuit culture, shamans were people who had great magical powers and knowledge. As

This inuksuk is "sacred" or "given as a gift." The photographer gave it two matches and wished for good weather for the rest of his travels. His wish was granted.

Above: Inuksuit can be a sacred connection to the past. One Inuk tells of feeling the comforting presence of his deceased parents when he visited two inuksuuk he remembers from his childhood.

Right: An Inuit woman with her baby on her back, photographed in 1931, fishes through a crack in the ice.

well as being able to converse with the spirit world, it was believed shamans could take flight when they wished to travel to other places.

There is a legend told by an Inuit elder about how two particular inuksuuk came to be. Two shamans were once coming from opposite directions and met in mid-air halfway between Igloolik and Repulse Bay. There they collided. When they first landed they exchanged news about their communities—who was sick, who had passed away, whether there was enough food and so on. Then they began to playfully wrestle with one another. Before they departed back to their camps, they each built an inuksuk to commemorate their encounter. These inuksuuk were as tall as a man, and were built from large rocks collected from the rolling hills of that area. Today, the inuksuk built by the Igloolik shaman remains standing, while the one built by the shaman from Repulse Bay has toppled. This is said to be because the shaman from Repulse Bay was the first to die.

ᓂᑭᕚᑐᖅᕚᓂ

NIKISUITTUQ
NORTH STAR

During the height of the arctic winter, the sun never rises and the stars are visible both day and night. The moon can circle the sky for days without setting. The moonlight shining across the snowy land makes it bright enough to see, even though there is no sun.

Closer to the North, the dark days get longer. Sometimes the sun doesn't show itself for many days, which means the nights are twenty-four hours long. (And during the peak of the summer, the sun never sets—making for around the clock light.) Even though the arctic winter is long, dark and cold, there is joy and wonder to be seen in the ever-changing northern lights, the aurora borealis.

An Inuit hunter in the mid-1900s comes into his snow house with a fox to feed his family.

Above: Mother and child are warm and snug in their caribou-skin bed.
Full page: A snow house glows from the light of a *qulliq* (a seal-oil lamp).

In the high latitude of the Arctic, the nearby North Pole's strong magnetic field draws solar particles to its skies. These charged particles interact with gases in the earth's atmosphere to create an awesome light show. As the aurora dances across the darkened skies, it moves and changes, appearing in many forms: a shining arc; a broad and brilliant band of color; a soft luminous glow in the sky; radiant filaments or streamers; or shimmering curtains, fans or flames.

Inuit tradition cautions you not to whistle at the northern lights since they will come closer and could cut off your head or carry you up to the sky. Some say that the spirits of people who die go to the northern lights, where they forever play football using a walrus head as the ball.

During the winter, many Inuit lived on the sea ice, where the seals lived. If enough game could be found to feed the people and fuel the *qulliit* (lamps), much of the winter was spent comfortably within the snow house. Food shortages, however, would bring fear and even starvation to the Inuit.

Throughout this dark time of year, the stars in the night sky were important to the Inuit. Their position in the sky was used to tell time and to predict the return of the spring sun. Hunters used the stars as points of reference in navigation.

Inuit built some inuksuit to point toward the North Star, *Nikisuittuq*, the star that does not move. This bright star appears high in the sky, its altitude above the horizon equal to the latitude of your position.

ᕴᑕᕐᒥ ᐃᓄᒃᔪᒃ

QILANGMI INUKSUK
INUKSUK IN THE SKY

Over just a few generations, the Inuit way of life has changed from an ancient hunting and fishing culture where communication was only possible by travelling on foot or by dog sled and kayak, to today's culture, where Inuit live in communities year round and communication is via snowmobile, airplane, telephone, television and computer.

While traditional stone inuksuit used as communication aids are still found throughout the North, new ways are also evolving. In 1990, the Anik B satellite was launched into orbit. In the Canadian North, a venture known as "The Inukshuk Project" uses this satellite to provide sophisticated communication links to the Inuit. This modern day "inuksuk" has enabled contemporary communication throughout the Arctic, through digital data, telephone and television images.

Land, sea and sky meet along the Arctic coastline.

In their traditional way of life, the Inuit stressed the value of respect for others, working together to achieve common goals and their vital connection to the land and its resources. The inuksuk remains as a symbol of this lifestyle. Today, this same symbol will guide the Inuit as they choose their path into the future.

Below: Inuit in the 1920s use telescopes to look into the distance. *Full page:* In the Arctic today, the snowmobile is often the transportation mode of choice.

BUILD YOUR OWN INUKSUK

ᐃᓕᖅᑯᓯ ᐃᓄᒃᓱᓕᐅᕈᑎᖕ

Above: Assembling a collection of different shapes of stones is the starting point for building any inuksuk.

Before you begin to build an inuksuk, study the shapes and stones of inuksuit shown in this book. As you now know, an inuksuk can be as simple as two stones near each other to show a direction along a path. A stack of several stones could serve as a message centre. Or perhaps you may decide to balance a long stone on top of several others to provide a pointer along a path.

First, you'll need to select suitable stones. If you live in a rocky area you might find stones nearby in a stone pile, a stone fence or by the roadside. Make sure to get permission before you pick rocks that are not on your own property. You can also get stones from a garden centre (where they are sold as decorative items for the garden) or from a rock quarry.

Choose stones that are easy to handle. Your inuksuk can be any size or shape that you like, much will depend on the rocks you choose. If you are building an inuksuk that is knee-height or smaller, your stones should be about the size of your hands and feet. If you plan to build a larger inuksuk, make sure that you have an adult helping to lift and balance the larger stones. You can build an inuksuk from any variety and number of stones; however, stones with flat tops and bottoms are the easiest to stack and keep balanced.

Choose a special spot for your inuksuk—perhaps along a walkway, as a centrepiece in your garden, next to your front door or beside a favorite resting place.

BUILDING AN INUNNGUAQ

ᖃᓄᖅ ᐃᓄᒃᓱᓚᐅᑎᓇᐊᒃᓴᖅ ᐃᓄᓐᖑᐊᓐᖑᔪᒥᒃ

1. To build a stone person, you will need at least 3 fat rocks (for the legs and head) and 3 to 5 flat stones for the body, arms and shoulder stones. You might also need a few very small stones to act as balancing wedges.

2. Begin by placing the 2 largest and fattest stones securely on the ground or on a flat stone platform. You may need to dig shallow holes in the ground so that they will sit securely. The top edge of the stones should be at about the same height, and set as far apart as the length of the largest flat stone you have.

3. Now balance the large flat stone on top of the leg stones. Move it around until it sits securely without wobbling (the stones have uneven surfaces so even minor shifts can help them to fit together better). If you need to, you can wedge a small stone between the larger ones to prevent wobbling.

4. Place the next largest flat stone on top. Gently shift it around until it feels secure.

arm stones while you put the shoulder stone on. The weight of the shoulder stone will help to keep the arms in place.

5 Choose the 2 smallest flat stones for the arms. Examine each arm stone to see which is the heaviest end. Place this end on top of the flat surface of the body stone, with the lighter end of the arm stone hanging out over the edge.

7 Now, choose a small round stone for the head. Carefully place this stone on top of the shoulder stone. If it feels a bit wobbly, pick it up, turn it around and replace it with a flatter side down.

This stone person is finished. If it falls apart, simply rebuild it trying to rebalance each stone. With practice, you will become very good at building an *inunnguaq* that is well balanced and sturdy.

6 When both arm stones are in place, put the flat shoulder stone on top of them. You may need a second person to hold the

Guide to Inuktitut Words

The Inuktitut language is written in symbols (syllabics) that represent a combination of sounds.

Common Inuktitut Sounds

ᐃ	**i** (ee, long e)	ᐅ	**u** (oo, u, long u)	ᐊ	**a** (ah)
ᐱ	**pi** (pee)	ᐳ	**pu** (poo)	ᐸ	**pa** (pah)
ᑎ	**ti** (tee)	ᑐ	**tu** (too)	ᑕ	**ta** (tah)
ᑭ	**ki** (kee)	ᑯ	**ku** (koo)	ᑲ	**ka** (kah)
ᒋ	**gi** (ghee)	ᒍ	**gu** (ghoo)	ᒐ	**ga** (ghah)
ᒥ	**mi** (me)	ᒧ	**mu** (moo)	ᒪ	**ma** (mah)
ᓂ	**ni** (nee)	ᓄ	**nu** (noo)	ᓇ	**na** (nah)
ᓯ	**si** (see)	ᓱ	**su** (soo)	ᓴ	**sa** (sah)
ᓕ	**li** (lee)	ᓗ	**lu** (loo)	ᓚ	**la** (lah)
ᔨ	**ji** (yee)	ᔪ	**ju** (yoo)	ᔭ	**ja** (yah)
ᕕ	**vi** (vee)	ᕗ	**vu** (voo)	ᕙ	**va** (vah)
ᕆ	**ri** (ree)	ᕈ	**ru** (roo)	ᕋ	**ra** (rah)
gutteral "k"					
ᕿ	**qi**	ᖁ	**qu**	ᖃ	**qa**
nasal "g"					
ᖏ	**ngi**	ᖑ	**ngu**	ᖓ	**nga**

There is no English equivalent for the following sound, but it is roughly "dsl."

ᖠ	**&i**	ᖢ	**&u**	ᖤ	**&a**

The letters in upper case indicate which syllable you put more emphasis on in pronouncing the word. Where there are no upper case letters, all syllables are evenly pronounced.

ᐊᓂᕐᓂᓕᒃ **Anirnilik** (Ah-NEK-nee-leek): has spirits or ghosts.

ᐊᐅᓚᖅᑯᑦ **Aulaqut** (OW-lah-khoot): an inuksuk used to make caribou run away.

ᐃᓄᐃᑦ **Inuit** (Ee-noo-eet): people or human beings. The word refers specifically to the people of the northern Arctic.

ᐃᓄᒃ **Inuk** (Ee-nook): person (the singular form of Inuit).

ᐃᓄᒃᓱᐃᑦ **Inuksuit** (Ee-nook-sweet): three or more stone markers (the plural form of inuksuk).

ᐃᓄᒃᓱᒃ **Inuksuk** (Ee-nook-sook): a stone marker that acts in the place of a human being.

ᐃᓄᒃᓱᒃᑲᑦ **Inuksukkat** (Ee-nook-sook-cut): many little inuksuit.

ᐃᓄᒃᓲᒃ **Inuksuuk** (Ee-nook-SOOHK): two stone markers.

ᐃᓄᒃᑎᑐᑦ **Inuktitut** (Ee-nook-tee-toot): the language of the Inuit people.

ᐃᓄᙱᐊᕐᒃ **Inunnguaq** (Ee-non-WAWK): something that resembles a person.

ᒪᒃᑖᖅ **Maktaaq** (Muk-TAAK): whale skin (the fleshy part including the outer layer and the skin right next to the fat, which is about an inch thick). It is a delicacy, sometimes boiled, but favored aged, or fresh and raw.

ᓇᒃᑲᑕᐃᑦ **Nakkatait** (Nah-cut-tait): things that fell in the water. An inuksuk with this name points to a good place to fish.

ᓇᖕᒋᐊᕐᐊᐅᑎᒥᒃ ᖃᐅᔨᒪᓕᑕᖅ **Nangiarautimik qaujimalitaq** (Nang-ee-ah-RAU-tee-mik Khau-yee-mah-li-tak): makes one aware of dangerous conditions.

ᓂᑭᓱᐃᑦᑐᖅ **Nikisuittuq** (Niki-sweet-TOK): never moves. This is also the word for the polestar, or North Star.

ᓂᕐᕿᑦ **Niqiit** (Nerk-heet): meats.

ᓂᐅᒡᕙᓕᕈᓗᐃᑦ **Niugvaliruluit** (NEWG-vah-lee-go-lo-eet): that has legs. An inuksuk with this name is built from stones piled on each other to form a window. Travellers look through the window to see the direction they should travel in.

ᓄᓇᕗᑦ **Nunavut** (Noo-nah-voot): our land. It is the name of the new territory in Arctic Canada.

ᐱᕈᔭᖃᕐᕕᒃ **Pirujaqarvik** (Pee-goo-yah-KHAK-vik): where the meat cache is.

ᖃᔭᒃᑯᕖᑦ **Qajakkuviit** (Kha-yak-koo-VEET): place for a kayak to be stored.

ᖃᔭᖅ **Qajaq** (KHAH-yahk): a light, narrow boat propelled by a double-bladed paddle (kayak).

ᖃᓪᓗᓈᑦ **Qallunaat** (Khad-low-NAAT): white (non-Inuit) people, European settlers.

ᕿᓚᖕᒥ **Qilangmi** (Khee-lang-mee): in the sky, or in the heavens.

ᖁᓪᓕᖅ **Qulliq** (Khud-lek): seal-oil lamp. The plural is ᖁᓪᓖᑦ **qulliit** (Khud-LEET).

ᖁᕕᐊᓱᒃᑐᖅ **Quviasuktuq** (Kho-vee-ah-sook-tok): expressing joy.

ᑐᒃᑐᑦ **Tuktut** (Took-TUT): caribou (plural). The singular is ᑐᒃᑐ **tuktu** (took-too). Caribou are also called ᑐᒃᑐᐃᑦ **tuktuit** (took-TWEET).

ᑐᐸᔭᖃᖕᐊᐅᑦ **Tupjakangaut** (Toob-jahk-hang-out): footprints of game. This inuksuk steers hunters toward good places to hunt.

ᐅᓗ **Ulu** (Oo-lu): Women's crescent-shaped knife. The ulu is a tool that has survived for thousands of years and is still widely used by Inuit women of all ages in everyday cutting, sewing and eating.

INDEX

Note: numbers in italics indicate captions